■ EASY START ■

Rob's caterpillar

Series editor: Keith Gaines

Illustrated by Margaret de Souza

Nelson

"I have found a caterpillar,"
said Rob.

"I am going to put it in this box."

"Let's give it some food,"
said Kim.
"Let's give it this plant."

4

"Let's make some holes in
the lid with this pin,"
said Rob.

The next day,

they looked in the box.

"Look at it now,"
said Kim.

"It is big and fat."

7

The next day,
they looked in the box.

"Look at it now,"
said Rob.

"It is sleeping in there,"
said Rob's Mum.
"We will go away and
let it sleep."

9

They looked in the box.

"Look at it now,"
said Kim.
"Look at it, Rob."

"We must let it go,"

said Rob's Mum.